Consider the Possibilities

Pursuing What Matters Most

MICHELE AIKENS

Dedication:

*To Ken Cheatham, friend, and coach, for teaching
me to think differently about what was in my hands.*

Table of Contents

Foreword

Warm, creative, kind, and engaging. These are the words that came to mind when I met Michele. We were both hired by a venture-capital-backed startup as executive coaches. Our role was to curate meaningful leadership discussions for women who were running companies, running departments, and in the midst of that, also running their personal lives.

What I learned later in our friendship is that Michele is uniquely created to help women, especially those over 50, remove the barriers to create pathways to what they desire most. She empowers them to step into their confidence gracefully.

Throughout this book, Michele leans into her lived experiences and coaching expertise to help readers understand that life's challenging experiences don't have to define them. Michele invites us to consider that at any time we can rewrite our life's manuscript with the possibility of creating an ending that is much better than what we could ever have imagined. Michele's writing is vulnerable, honest, and most of all, she sees you. You will feel connected to her like you would a long-time friend. Not one to inspire without motivating action, Michele invites the reader to reflect on thought-provoking questions to inspire insight and ideas on how to move forward.

Dear Reader, I'm excited that you will have an opportunity to experience Michele's warm heart and desire to serve others through each chapter. I promise you will leave inspired with a vision of your life's possibilities.

Nicole Johnson-Scales
CEO, NJS Consulting Group
& Design Your Professional Joy Coaching

Introduction

We have become a generation of performers. Whether taking pictures to share on social media or building a brand through creating a following, so much of what we do is "being on" for an audience. I recently attended a wedding where many were using their cameras to videotape portions rather than just being in the moment. I understand, I think. It is as if displaying my activities for others to see validates that I am in fact enjoying life. Or at least, I look like I'm enjoying it, so follow me. But one day something happens to destroy the illusion. Whether it is the loss of a job, the death of a spouse, a debilitating illness or something else, the formulas we trusted to keep ourselves no longer work. The excellent leader still lost his job in the buyout. Divorce or the loss of a spouse means the end of the relationship and connections that gave identity. Recovering from an illness may have left some with diminished physical function. The empty nest and deceased parent(s) suggest an emptiness of purpose – "Who am I if no one needs me?"

As if that wasn't enough, in 2020 we experienced the effects of a worldwide pandemic on our health, finances, homes, relationships, and our mental and emotional states. Many lost sources of income, faith in the political system, the connection of family and friends, and sadly, hope for what the future could look like. I think you get the picture.

Today, in a world connected by the internet, we are more disconnected than ever. As we perform for others, we have lost track of ourselves. Anxiety and depression are on the rise as many grapple with the life conflicts that keep us awake at night, or in bed during the day. Even in successful business undertakings, there is the nagging sense that something is missing, that there must be more. The daily work of treading water, no matter how beautiful the beach, is not enough. In fact, we take vacations to escape the lives we live, only to return eight days later to resume those lives. We are full and tanned, yet still hopeless. Physically rested but emotionally exhausted, we ask, "Is this all?"

Whatever the reason for your lack of hope, this book is designed to ignite the fire of possibility within you. In the next eight chapters, we will look at common mindsets that defeat optimism and give you tools to overcome them. I know that you are tired of trying and might feel hopeless about the possibility of your own success in business, relationships or achieving the life you were meant to live.

I pray that you will not accept defeat, but that you will *consider the possibilities* open to you and begin living the next phase of your life. Get up one more time, and let's journey together.

Chapter 1

There Are No Accidental Optimists

Have you ever met a person who was born with a sunny disposition and 60 years later, their disposition was still sunny and bright? Neither have I. I do not believe optimists are born; I believe they are made. Nobody accidentally becomes an optimist. Optimism is something that is chosen over circumstances, failures and disappointment.

What are you choosing today? If you are going to live life *considering the possibilities*, you must choose optimism. There will always be openings to focus on the worst thing that can happen, or who will be disappointed if you make a wrong choice. However, to *consider the possibilities,* you must contemplate the open doors that lie ahead of you if you are bold enough to pursue them. Some opportunities await you, but you can only see them through the eyes of optimism and hope.

Optimism is defined by Merriam-Webster's dictionary as, "an inclination to put the most favorable construction upon actions and events or to anticipate the best possible outcome."

What does optimism look like in your current situation? Would it be someone singing, "The sun will come out tomorrow?" Is it putting on a false, sunny face for the world to see while you grimace inwardly? According to the definition, optimism is an inclination– leaning towards a point of view that expects the best possible outcome, not the worst. As you consider your situation, what point of view are you leaning towards? Do you anticipate the best possible outcome, or the worst imaginable ending?

Considering the possibilities means you must decide to believe that what you are attempting can turn out well. When we consider a direction, we can approach it in one of two ways: expecting to encounter hindrances and opposition that will lead to failure or anticipating the best possible outcome. This means we can believe in a positive outcome for our journey, even if that outcome isn't exactly what we want.

Why do we choose to believe the worst possible outcome? Perhaps experience has shaped your outlook on what is possible for you. A series of "failures" may give you the impression that failure is the best you can do. Repeated disappointments can negatively affect our ability to hope. We "lose hope" and don't even look for a positive outcome.

We also fail to consider that good can come to us because of the word's others have spoken to, or about us. Were you compared to someone who didn't achieve success with words like, "You're just like _____? He wasn't smart either." Or how about this one, "Are you trying that again? I thought you would have moved on after the last time." And here is my favorite: "Are you sure you can do that?" Whoever said, "Sticks and stones may break my bones, but words can never hurt me," lied. Words can hurt deeply, especially if the source of those words is a trusted person like a parent, teacher, minister, or role model.

One of the reasons words can and do hurt so deeply is because our words are creative – they produce the world we experience, even though our potential might be vastly different from the world we are living in. As a child, from approximately kindergarten through the third or fourth grade, I was a stutterer. In certain situations, it was difficult for me to speak without stuttering. There are a few reasons this could have started, but my wise mother applied an unexpected solution: she put me in a church group created to train public speakers. You see, even though I stuttered in class and in one-on-one conversations, I did not stutter while saying a prepared speech at church. My mother knew there was a speaker inside me that did not stutter. As I practiced with the group, I found the confidence to take a breath, think about what I wanted to say, and articulate it publicly. Today, I rarely get nervous speaking before crowds, no matter the size, and I have not stuttered in at least half a century.

Had I continued to behave and experience "being a stutterer", my life would have lined up around that description. I would have limited any opportunities for verbal engagement, and not considered any career that would involve a lot of talking with people. That is not to say I wouldn't have a good life, but it would not be the life I have now. My mother created an experience that validated the speaker and not the stutterer.

The descriptors (words) of me changed and created a new outcome.

What words come to mind when you think of yourself? To experience the possibilities available to you, you must examine your description of yourself. What relative do you most resemble physically? What words do you use to describe that relative? Who are the people you are compared to? What words are used in those comparisons? Now here is the important question: do those words ring true in the deepest part of your mind, will or emotions? Do those words create feelings of anxiety, 'butterflies,' anger, irritation, sadness, or hopelessness?

I believe we all have an Inner Compass (IC), a personal GPS that directs us away from or towards the places we need to be. If we are performing in life, or preoccupied with work, family concerns or reputation-building, we may become accustomed to ignoring our Inner Compass while we pursue other things. These may be good things, and they can also be distractions from where our Inner Compass is trying to direct us.

Action Step: Stop and still your thoughts for 10 minutes. Write five words that you or others have used to describe you. Do you agree with those words as descriptors of you? If not, write five words that resonate with your spirit as descriptors of you, even if you do not see them actively in your life. Remember the example of my mother. The human descriptor of me was "stutterer," but she saw a speaker. She chose to follow the compass that affirmed the speaker and not the stutterer. Once you have written the words that resonate with your spirit, note any differences between words you or others have used to describe you in the past.

Practice: Replace the words others have used to describe you with those that resonate within your spirit whenever you describe yourself. Mentally correct those former words when you find yourself using them in your thoughts about yourself.

Words I or others have used to define me.

_____

_____

_____

_____

Words that resonate with me about I really am.

_____

_____

_____

_____

_____

Chapter 2

Yep, What's Happening Now Will Change Life as You Know It

L et's admit it, whatever you might be facing right now is tough and may even seem insurmountable from your current perspective. Whether you are dealing with the loss of a job, a relationship or an ability, things will not be the same anymore. Take a deep breath. Take another if you must. Do not run away from what is happening; do not revert to familiar coping mechanisms or distractions. Practicing optimism does not mean disconnecting from reality. Stop and look into the face of what I call, "The Big It."

What do you see? Often when we investigate "The Big It," we see a reflection of our own insecurities. "Did this fail because I wasn't good enough? Maybe if I had been smarter (or not so smart), nicer (or tougher), less confrontational (or willing to fight), "The Big It" might not have happened. "The Big It" sends us back to our defaults of fear, rejection, or inadequacy. When we look at "The Big It" through the eyes of these things, we might come away with a sense that we deserve what has happened. This thing that is happening to us is what we get for not being good enough.

If we continue down this path, we will begin to shrink in size and courage in relation to "The Big It." Our thoughts of why "It" is happening remind us of every failed attempt, perceived rejection, and sense of inadequacy. As "The Big It" grows proportionate to our fears, we lose track of the things we did right, the successes both large and small, the accepting and fulfilling relationships we have with people who are aware that we aren't perfect, but that we are enough. If something doesn't halt it, "The Big It" will begin to wield its physical strength: keeping us in bed, preventing forward movement, causing headaches, crying spells, tense muscles, and weight gain (or loss) to name a few. If we allow it, "The Big It" will empty us of our beliefs that there are new possibilities until we become a shell of the place where hope once lived.

Does that sound like you? I get it. "The Big It" happened to me in October of 2009. I was the publisher of a magazine that was on the verge of national success. I was working my dream job; using my knowledge of publishing to inspire women. The December 2009 issue of the magazine featured Taraji P. Henson on the cover. After five years of working with a part-time editor and a staff of volunteer writers, that magazine was scheduled to hit store shelves all around the country. When the company couldn't pay my full salary, I ignored the signs – I pressed on, passionately convinced that my sacrifice would pay off with success that would make up for the sacrifices of others who had worked on the magazine and increase the company's bottom line. Through a series of decisions in our parent company, the magazine was eliminated in October – right on the verge of success.

What followed for me was two years of keeping a straight-faced façade while wrestling with depression and a major identity crisis. As the eldest child, I was taught to care for people I was responsible for. At least two writers and an editor dropped out of the faith community we were all a part of. I felt personally responsible for their pain.

13

Not only was I obviously not a decent magazine publisher, but I couldn't even take care of those who trusted me with their gifts. "The Big It" shut me down for two years, even though I went through the motions of job hunting, going to church, and convincing everyone that I was strong enough to handle it. To those closest to me, however, it was a different story. My friend Betty told me at one point that I sounded like an old Chi-Lites song (maybe Have you seen her....), another friend told me "If you want another job, just get one." My husband watched helplessly, probably not knowing what to say for the better part of two years. I kept going through the motions every day though because I had two children and I know they were watching me. Not for myself, but for them; I felt I needed to demonstrate how to deal with devastating failure.

Even that wasn't enough to defeat "The Big It." Consider the following writing exercise that I now use in one of my author coaching classes. This exercise is designed to help writers stretch their imaginations by giving voice and emotion to an inanimate object. This is what my couch could have said about me those two years. If the sofa could talk....

Here she comes again. It must be morning. Why can't she sit somewhere else? Every day for two years, she has come and sat right here. I've developed a sunken place on the right cushion, and my arm is wearing on that side. I can usually tell what kind of day it's going to be by the way she walks downstairs. If she shuffles slowly, she is going to lie down and watch movies. If she walks quickly, she is going to search for a job on the computer until her hopes get dashed. Sometimes, she sits here and cries. Other times, she desperately searches for jobs on the computer for hours. There are days she just watches movies. I hear her pray while she's looking for work, but then, she collapses into tears after a couple of hours.

Today, she answered the phone. I cannot tell who she's talking to, but they talked a long time. She got up and started to walk as she talked. This is different. I haven't seen her so animated. When she got off the phone, she prayed, got her computer, and moved her butt from me to the dining room. Something changed today.

What changed for me? We'll talk about that in a later chapter. For now, let's keep unpacking how your "Big It" is affecting you.

Action Step: What "Big It" has changed your life? Can you put into words what you believed about yourself because of the "Big It?" Look back to the words that resonate with your spirit in Chapter 1. Do those words agree with what you believe about yourself because of the "Big It?" What can you do today to express more of the words that resonate with your spirit?

What is my "Big It," using as few words as possible?

_____

What has changed in my beliefs about me since the "Big It?"

_____

Is this the first time you have felt this way?

Yes ☐   **No** ☐

Chapter 3

Consider the Possibilities If You Unhooked Yourself from Mindsets That Hide Opportunities

What did you have for breakfast this morning? How often have you had that same breakfast in the past month, the past year, the past ten years? I eat oatmeal occasionally because it is supposed to be good for you – not because it is tasty. One day, my daughter made oatmeal, which I normally eat with fruit, with savory seasonings instead. AND IT WAS AMAZING. Who would have thought that oatmeal could taste like something I would actually want? We all have them: mindsets and habits we have engaged in for so long that we cannot remember life before they existed. My oatmeal story is an example of a mindset we deal with every day.

An unchallenged mindset can be like how I looked at oatmeal. It is what you do because you're supposed to, but it is not supposed to be enjoyable. Perhaps you are working a job that provides a salary, but no mental stimulation or challenge. You may have reached the top of your possibilities in the workplace, so you aren't even at work (in your head) for big chunks of the day. What can you do? You get up and go to work every day because "at least I have a job." What other things are you doing because mentally "at least" it is better than something else?

Let's examine the phrase, "At least I have," to uncover what's happening inside our heads. Here's a small English lesson to reacquaint you with word meaning and context. Least in this phrase is a modifier or advert to the phrase, "I have." Least by definition is "smallest in amount, extent or significance." How often have you justified staying in a mentally unstimulating or emotionally painful place because "to the smallest extent, it is a place to be?" Are you in a miserable relationship because "by the smallest amount, I have someone?" Do you continue living well below your potential at work or school because "this is the smallest amount of significance I am capable of?"

How many activities or relationships are you in because of "at least?" Take mental inventory of the ways you use "at least". Whether it is a loveless marriage, a dead-end job, or a hamster wheel of mindless activity, what is the "at least" that keeps you locked into less than who you were created to be? What "at least" keeps you longing to do, but unable to move? What is the "at least" that prevents you from confronting what needs to change?

The phrase "at least" means you have settled for far less than what you are capable of accomplishing. You have compromised for "just enough" and made peace with that dull ache in the middle of your chest. I'm talking about the dull ache or sensation you get when you consider visiting another country or creating adventure through a new business or project. That ache reminds you that you have already said, "no," to those things somewhere inside of you.

The "Who" You Were Created to Be

The phrase, "who you were created to be," may have raised an eyebrow. I don't believe any of us are cosmic gambles, randomly assigned to life without clues to the meaning of our existence. I do believe that we are all born with gifts, abilities and temperaments that will lead us to who we are created to be if we pay attention. I believe in the intelligent design of the universe, from the largest solar system to the smallest cell.

You are no exception when it comes to the intelligence of your design. Inside you is a universe of possibilities, and to discover them, you must examine that universe, or do what I call, "looking into your toolbox." Your toolbox consists of the things you do well without much training, the ideas that fuel your passion, your history and your way of learning and relating to others. Just like you can identify a doctor or a plumber by what's in his or her toolbox, exploring your toolbox will point to your own possibilities.

Where Do You Naturally Shine?

Have you ever watched children at play? Curiosity often leads them to a toy that teaches or affirms a strength. My daughter could play with building blocks for hours while my son preferred watching Barney and listening to story time tapes. Today, my daughter is a producer who as a youngster, literally built her own contraptions to learn the craft. My son is a professional actor who coaches actors and creates success stories. As a child, my hobbies were reading and writing stories. My husband, now a financial officer for several non-profits, was treasurer of his high school class. The examples are all around us and especially visible in our families.

There were some things you were naturally good at as a child. You didn't have to work hard to give a speech, draw a great picture, or influence other children to engage in mischief. Whatever your thing was, it came naturally to you. Try to remember what you enjoyed doing as a child; do you see connections to those activities or skills in your adult world?

If you don't see those connections right away, that's ok. Sometimes the things we enjoyed and were good at did not seem useful to the adults in our world, so they may have encouraged us to "do something practical" instead. Our Inner Compass – the guidance system, will use our curiosity and natural gifts to lead us to where we belong – unless the compass gets tinkered with. We'll talk more about that later.

What Are You Passionate About?

Outside of your family, what matters most to you in the world? If you never had to be concerned about money or paying bills again, what would you devote your life to? While the answer to this may vary depending on your age and other things, an examination of this question could point to a potential direction. There are places in our world that need the touch of healers, builders, teachers, or partners. Identifying what you are passionate about – what keeps you awake at night or gets you up in the morning – will direct you to places where you have been designed to make a difference.

As children, we often hear the fun things we want to do are not practical as we grow up. As adults, too, we can get talked out of our zest for life. If you say you want to go to another country and dig wells so citizens there can have clean water, you might hear, "What about the people here? Why can't you just help them?" Or if someone wants to leave a great job to work with disadvantaged children, I have heard the argument, "You can help them more by staying in your job and funding an organization that is already doing that."

These arguments say, "Your passion is not practical. Be a grownup and put those dreams away." Your zest for life is part of the spark that is you, and you were created to make a difference in the world. Identifying ideas and causes you are passionate about are important items in your toolbox.

How Do You Express Yourself?

Are you outgoing and friendly, quiet and introspective, or a combination of both? Whether you identify as extroverted, introverted, or one of the in-between categories, consider your preferred way of expression as you identify the possibilities in your life. Your preferred way of expressing yourself could be in music, writing, speaking or the arts. Your preferred way of expression is different from your learned way of expression. We learn how to express ourselves based on circumstances and environment. If you are surrounded by yelling and screaming, you will learn to express yourself that way. If you are surrounded by those who go "radio silent" rather than discuss issues, you will learn not to express too much of yourself. If assumptions were made about you growing up and you took those assumptions as truth, you may have limited how you express yourself.

For instance, as a child books were a constant companion to me, whether at home, in the car, or when my parents visited friends. By the time I finished eighth grade, I was reading at the rate of a late high school senior or first-year college student. I didn't set out to get high scores; I simply enjoyed a good story (and I still do). How did this love of reading develop? I was plagued with chronic bronchitis as a child, so I didn't get to play outside as much as other children. I could go to the library and check out four books at a time, though. I later skipped a grade in Jr. High, which added to my social awkwardness. On the outside, I fit the profile of a "bookworm:" an introvert who prefers the company of books to people. When I started working as an adult, my second real job was in public relations, and it was fun!!! I liked the energy of preparing conferences, commercial shoots, and anything else that was public. The whole time, I maintained my image of a bookworm, assuming that my enthusiasm for the field was me putting on a mask to do my job. While I do enjoy books in many forms, I am also energized by a crowd. I wasn't wearing a mask when I eagerly engaged in public relations activities – I was expressing myself authentically. Growing up, I didn't have opportunities to express that part of my personality, so I didn't realize it even existed.

As we age, the opportunities for greater expression are only limited if you believe change is impossible. Like my bookworm example, you may have kept yourself in a "box" simply because you never had the opportunity to express yourself in new ways. Today, right now, you can begin to learn new ways of expressing yourself. I look at the popularity of "Paint and Sip" parties and realize some of us love the idea of expressing ourselves through art. Someone saw the possibilities of creating a way for others to "speak artistically" and created an industry around it. If you have always wanted to speak on a public stage but were afraid to, explore a speaking class or a group like Toastmasters. Just because you have learned to express yourself in a particular way doesn't mean you can't learn new ways.

Pause for a moment and consider ways of expression that you have always wanted to try but were afraid to do so. I still remember being scolded in kindergarten for coloring outside the lines. For a good part of life before 50, I worked ridiculously hard to conform to what was expected; to somehow put my outside-the-lines personality into a form that others would be comfortable with. While others were comfortable, I felt restricted most of the time. We need people who color inside the lines; they make sure we follow the rules and that all the trains stay on the track. We also need people who color outside the lines. They build the cities for the trains and their tracks to run on.

How can you express yourself in a way that you have always wanted to try? What's stopping you?

Is Your Compass Broken?

I mentioned an inner compass earlier. I have never been a hiker because I didn't know anyone who hiked, and I was always very afraid of getting lost. One day while researching for a presentation about directions, I discovered how a compass works. I will share this explanation from campsmartly.com:

> "Compasses use magnetism to ensure accuracy. Every compass is set to magnetic north. Compasses have a magnetized needle pointing out from the center that

aligns itself with the horizontal aspect of the Earth's natural magnetic field. Because this magnetic field exists, it exerts a torque on the special magnetic needle to pull it north. No matter how much you move or spin a compass, the needle will always settle into its equilibrium orientation— north will always be north."

I found this FASCINATING because I learned that a compass works because it is tied to the earth's natural magnetic field- not to your state of "lostness." This means that when you are lost, you can trust the compass even when the surroundings are unfamiliar.

You were born with a built-in compass made of your gifts (those things you do naturally well), a zest for life to fuel those gifts, and a way of expression that directs those gifts. Even when you feel lost and vulnerable, learning and trusting your IC will help you to literally find your way. This is why it is important to mentally get off the hamster wheel periodically and check your location. Have you lost sight of what you do well? Is it hard to find a joyful expression of what matters to you? You may have a broken compass.

To carry the compass analogy just a little further, when the needle of a compass points in the wrong direction, campers say it has become depolarized. The most likely cause of this depolarization is that the compass has been affected by another magnetic source. Remember the compass was already aligned with the earth's magnetic field, so the second magnetic source caused the compass to malfunction. So, what happens when your IC encounters another force that causes it to misfunction? Like the hiker with a broken compass, we get lost. Some forces that can cause your IC to malfunction include:

- Words spoken at a pivotal time that change your view and direction of who you are or can be.
- Events that cause you to choose safety and acquiescence over courage and adventure.
- Systems (racial, political, gender, age, business, family) that limit you to a certain space or expression.
- False loyalties that require you to stay in a small place, so others don't feel uncomfortable.

Recovering your direction means you must take some steps to repair your IC.

Identify and eliminate the source that caused the dysfunction. Do you have a sense inside yourself of "uneasy peace?" Uneasy peace could be an indicator of compromise. If you are compromising the directive of your IC because of negative words, an event, hurdles in a system or relationship loyalties, consider this. What would happen if for one week you made a small step in the direction your IC is pointing to?

Start making the repairs to your IC. To repair your IC, you must lessen its exposure to the things that cause it to dysfunction. If the words you have been acting on go against the wisdom of your compass, prepare a statement that confronts those words, and then repeat that statement every time the negative words confront the wisdom of your IC. The statement can be a favorite saying, a scripture, or something you create yourself, but repairing the compass means replacing words or thoughts that conflict with your inner compass.

If an event made you afraid to courageously pursue the direction of your IC, take the time to consider what the event said to you about your possibilities. For example, if you have experienced the loss of a spouse through death or divorce, but are afraid to consider connecting with another, is it because you believe your time for a loving relationship has passed? Or do you consider it disloyal to a former spouse to open yourself to another loving relationship? What direction is your IC pointing to? Is there a conflict?

Do you feel limited by a system, whether it is business, racial, gender, age, family or some other structure? Here's an important question, do you agree that the judgments of that system are true? It will be difficult to overcome the limits of a system if you agree that those limits are appropriate. For instance, much of my business includes working with people over 50 to create new opportunities for business and personal fulfillment. If I believed the enjoyment of life ended at 50, and that value to workplace was lessened for those over 50, then I would not be able to do what I do. The fact is I believe possibilities for a fulfilling life grow as we age if we are courageous enough to pursue them. I also believe that should you decide to work, your experience and perspective increase your value to the workplace exponentially. That's why it is so easy for me to "buck any system" that says otherwise.

Learn to trust where the IC is directing you. This simply means weigh what you hear and sense in your heart about the next steps or changes while considering the items in your toolbox that we discussed in this chapter. After quiet and careful consideration, create a plan to implement the changes wisely and realistically. Finally, take the first step.

Get comfortable making adjustments. As you explore where your IC directs you, you might make a misstep or two. You may even miss it altogether. We have gotten out of the habit of quietly listening to our IC, so you may hear directions that are influenced by some of the other factors mentioned above. The wonderful thing about adjusting is that anything you learned when you got off course can be used once you get back on course. For example, if you started a business that "failed," you now have loads of intelligence that will help you in your next venture. You can, according to Leadership Coach John Maxwell, "Fail forward."

Chapter 4

Consider the Possibilities If You Actually…Change?

Hmm. Let's think about that for 30 seconds. When faced with possibilities for your life if you are willing to make changes, why is our second response (after the initial enthusiasm) often, "What if I can't?" This thought comes after the empowerment workshop is over or the sermon has ended. The music has stopped, the lights are off, and the crowd is gone. You sit alone with the idea of change and wonder "What was I thinking to believe I could actually be that person?"

The way we live our lives reminds me in so many ways of the movie, The Matrix. In case you haven't seen it, the movie illustrates life from two perspectives. One group consists of those who live plugged into a machine while being fed the dream of life. The other group are those living a life that is hard but has a purpose and is not a dream.

Those living a real-life can visit the world of dreams (The Matrix), but those living in The Matrix can never experience reality.

The idea of possibilities for a different way of living can be so intimidating that we plug back into a "matrix" of our own. In this matrix, we wake up every morning and do what we've always done: take care of children and home, go to work, endure the micro-assaults on our possibilities for something different, come home and have dinner, go to sleep, and wake up to do the same thing the next day. Any deviation from the established norm sends alarm bells off to our friends, families, and most of all, ourselves. We run back to what is "safe" and familiar, even if our Inner Compass is pointing wildly in another direction.

What is your idea of "safety?" Is it having a home where you are protected from the elements and safe from predators? That's a good example. Does that idea of safety extend to your financial health? Your emotional health? In every area of our lives, what is considered "safe" has different connotations. If your home is physically secure, but your finances are stretched beyond their means, you may not feel safe from fear even if the alarm is on and all the locks are working. This kind of safety is different from physical safety; it is what many refer to as insecurity.

Insecurity has a couple of definitions, one of them being, "the state of being open to danger or threat; lack of protection." When we attempt to try something new or step out of a box that we have been put into, there are threats and the possibility of danger to our daily lives, our relationships, and our reputations. These are some hindrances; "Am I able to do this?" "Will people accept me?" "Will I look like a fool?" Just like in the Matrix movie, embracing change is a process that can be painful, but is well within your power to achieve. Here are six stages that will help you understand the process of change.

Stage 1- Loss of Security: This is the stage in which you admit there will be a sense of loss of security regardless of whether or not you perceive the change to be good or bad. There is safety in knowing exactly what needs to be done on the job where you've worked 20 years. You can probably do it with your eyes closed. . In this kind of safety, you don't have to think too hard or challenge your expectations. If, however, you decide to make changes, you will likely feel uncomfortable, uncertain, and unglued. These feelings of insecurity are normal and to be expected whether the change is a good one (you got a promotion) or a challenging one (you got a divorce). At each stage you can choose to move forward into the discomfort or retreat into safety.

Stage 2- Self-Doubt: This is the stage in which all comfort is lost. As you doubt the facts, you struggle to find information about the change that you believe is valid. Your thinking is skewed with unbelief, antagonism, resentment, skepticism, and blame.

It might be in this next stage that the safety net is gone. You have moved into a new job where NOTHING is comfortable. Although you were the expert at your last job, you are now the newbie, flailing in a sea of new rules, corporate culture, and your own insecurity. Perhaps, you left a job to start your own business and are now wondering if you did the right thing. You must learn to do business if you are going to pay your mortgage, but "WHAT WERE YOU THINKING?" Suddenly, you "remember" that you aren't good with people and don't know how to sell. Fear reaches a crescendo unrivaled by anything you have ever experienced. You either keep moving forward or find a safe place. This is also when you might want to pick a fight with your Inner Compass. You will recognize this is happening when you start to use the same words against yourself that others have used against you.

Stage 3- Loss of Comfort: This stage brings discomfort. The discomfort of change now becomes clear and starts to settle in. This stage is full of frustration and lethargy.

As you start to settle in with the decisions you've made, you know you must move either forward or back. I remember the time I bought a lovely red sports car. The salesman did a good job of selling it because I bought a car I didn't know how to drive- it had a manual transmission. I got enough of a driving lesson from the salesman to get the car home, and then I was on my own. I remember crying the first night because I didn't know what it took to get that car up a hill. I looked out of the window the next day, a Saturday, and wondered, "What have I done? I bought a car I can't drive. Woe is me!" And then I started wondering how I was going to get to work on Monday. That's when I knew I had to make a choice to either call the dealer and tell him I didn't want the car or learn how to drive a car with a manual transmission today. I got into the car and drove it until I got comfortable, and by Sunday evening I was proficient.

According to Bill Eckstrom and Sara Wirth, "The best leaders were unique in their coaching and we could see that- either intentionally or unintentionally- they created or embraced an environment of discomfort as a growth mechanism (The Coaching Effect, page 16)." We grow the most through uncomfortable, chaotic situations.

The Pivotal Zone: The Pivotal Zone represents the place where you make the choice to either return to Stage 1 out of fear or move on to Stage 4 to discover the possibilities change has presented.

This is a deciding point in your move to change. It is in this stage that you get to decide what to do with the discomfort- go back to where it's comfortable or learn to drive a stick shift. In fact, the Pivotal Zone is like that pause between going from one gear to another in a manual transmission car.

Stage 4- Finding New Identity: This energizing stage is full of anticipation, perspective, and willingness to make decisions that give a new sense of hope and control for your life. You are optimistic about the outcome because of the choices now available.

"I really can drive a stick"! That's what it feels like when you get to stage four. You have learned some things about yourself and your possibilities. Perhaps you made your first sale or finished the manuscript. Maybe you now know that the failure of a business or relationship does not make you a failure. You can see new possibilities in front of you because you have done the hard work of confronting uncertainty and learning new skills and ways of being.

Stage 5- Fulfilling the Call: The fifth state is one of courage where you understand the change and are confident of what you can accomplish.

Your Internal Compass was steering you toward an idea or opportunity that would stretch you and utilize the best of what is in your toolbox. You can now look back and understand why it was necessary to change, and you may even begin to appreciate some of the hardest lessons and wild emotional swings you experienced on the journey to this stage.

Stage 6- Call to Action: In this final stage you have regained your ability and willingness to be flexible. You have new insights into the changes and the rewards and consequences- past, present and future.

The wonderful and scary thing about this stage is that as you develop confidence and willingness, you may find yourself right back at stage 1: getting ready for the next adventure and opportunity for learning.

So, where are you in the stages of change? To say that you can't change is a myth that perhaps you have chosen to believe. What may be truer is that you are at a point of change and must decide to move forward or remain where you are. Each stage of change brings both unique challenges and opportunities to shift your view of the possibilities in your own life. At each stage, you can choose to stand still and experience none of the possibilities available to you. You have a choice in this; no matter how others are affected, you are in charge of the decision to move into each stage of change.

Homework- You are here: Plot your location on the Change Map below. What experiences or "landmarks" help you to identify which stage of change you are in? Identify the feelings you have as you consider your journey through change.

Loss of Security	Self-Doubt ?	Loss of ⚠ Comfort

Finding new identity	The Pivotal Zone	Fulfilling the call	✈ Call to Action

Chapter 5

Consider the Possibilities:
That You Were Made for Greater
Than What You Currently See

As a child raised in a Christian home, I was taught to be polite and humble. That meant I should never talk too much about myself, always listen to others' stories and "walk in their shoes" if possible so that I could empathize with their plights in greater measure. As a "nerd" growing up, my childhood and teenage years were spent hiding the fact that I was smart so that I didn't get teased about "talking" or "acting white." What a shame that in a time where brainpower is needed the most, the analytical-leaning children are encouraged that something else (athletic prowess, street-savvy, or entertainment activities) is deemed more valuable and worthy of esteem by society in general. To avoid appearing arrogant and self-serving, I intentionally "dumbed down" and went overboard to push others into the spotlight, while avoiding it myself.

The spotlight is a funny thing though – it knows who belongs on stage and whose time has not yet come. We talked about your Inner Compass in chapter 1. Your Inner Compass will lead you into the spotlight created for you to shine when it is time. However, the way you see yourself could make you shrink back from the possibilities designed for you. If you are like me, for example, not talking too much about yourself (or your business) will prevent you from letting others know how you can benefit them. You won't sell your services effectively because doing so requires that you confidently present your strengths to others. My friend and coach, Ken Cheatham, says that whether you are in business or just in life, you are in sales. Whether you are making a presentation for your product or service or outlining a case for a strengthened relationship, you must understand and be confident that you bring value to the relationship.

If you have been taught not to say too much about yourself so that you don't appear arrogant, you need to make some adjustments. Let's look at some definitions from Cambridge Dictionary.

Arrogant: unpleasantly proud and behaving as if you are more important than, or know more than other people

Confident: being certain of your abilities or having trust in people, plans, or the future

***

Arrogant behavior says, "Move because I'm the star." Confident behavior says, "There is room for both of us to chine." Both of these words give insight into how we treat ourselves and others. If you are arrogant, here's a newsflash, you are not better than anyone else. You may know more, have more money, live in a different neighborhood, or work in a higher-paying profession, but you are no better than another. If you lack confidence, here's your newsflash: You are not less than anyone else. You may not know as much, might have less money, live in "the wrong" neighborhood, or be unemployed. You may have less, but you are not less. Take a few seconds to let that sink in.

While these are things I learned as a child, they are not childish thoughts. Your value includes your experiences, struggles, talents, scars, and strengths. Both arrogance and lack of confidence because of what you have experienced will hinder your ability to perceive the direction of your Inner Compass. You might also over or underestimate your ability to accomplish a goal based on arrogant or timid inner self-talk. Both extremes are filters through which you will view your possibilities for change. Here is an acronym that will help clean the filter of how you look at your possibilities. The acronym uses the word VALUE.

View your possibilities considering the needs of the world. If you take the focus off of your insufficiencies and failures, what experiences do you have that can benefit someone else?

Allow yourself to go into the "back of your mental closet" and look at some ideas or plans you have put away. Think about those that are relevant to a problem you would like to solve, and that you would implement if resources were not a deterrent. Pause for a minute to see what is happening inside of you. Do you sense symmetry or a connection with the idea? If so, sit with the idea for a while longer to see what happens. Make notes about your thoughts if that will help.

Look into your toolbox. What skills, education, or emotional leanings do you have that relate to the ideas above. Look at your resources- financial, human and time. Do you have the resources and tools to work on the idea? If you don't have those resources, what would it take to get them? Sit for a while longer with this and pay attention to what is happening inside your heart. Do you sense excitement, curiosity, foreboding or something else? Add these thoughts to your notes.

Understand that starting a new project or idea will involve some risks and requires some discipline. Evaluate the risks and decide if you are willing to take them. Ask yourself what in your life needs to change to exercise the discipline you will need. Realistically consider the personal cost of making those changes.

Execute! We all know how to make plans, identify goals, and evaluate risks. Once the thinking and planning are done, you still must do something. Move!

Chapter 6

Consider the Possibilities: That It's Not Too Late and You're Not Too Old

How did you mark your last birthday? Did you celebrate excitedly with people who matter to you (and perhaps some that don't matter as much)? Did you spend the day pampering or taking care of yourself? Did you sadly consider the years that have passed or wonder if your life has, so far, been wasted? While some of us look at each birthday like a personal New Year, others may view the day with trepidation and even regret. As a girl and teen, I heard the message repeated: "Never tell your age." I had a teacher in high school who said, "If a woman will tell her age, she'll tell anything." These words – barriers to embracing aging – still shape how many view the passage of time. These words tell us not to acknowledge outwardly that we have lived years and learned lessons, but to cultivate the appearance of "eternal youth". Seriously though, what would that look like – being forever 27? No thanks!

As we talk about our response to growing older, we must acknowledge the big glaring bias in our society – no, not that one. The age one. We live in a youth-obsessed society, and quite frankly always have. Twenty-five- to 34-year-olds didn't just become a coveted advertising target; products have always targeted the youngest adults in society to pitch their wares. With so much media buzz aimed at younger audiences, those outside that demographic can feel left out and unnecessary, or at least that's the way it used to be.

I'm talking about advertising because much of what we believe about our society and ourselves comes through the messaging of advertising and media. I'm happy to see that images of older adults are no longer projected as frail, comical figures. Even with "sexy, upbeat senior images" our individual mindsets still have to confront the stereotype that says after 55 you should start to "coast" towards retirement and death. I suspected that was the attitude towards, aging but watching the journey of the "Over 50s" to "Elsewhere" in the movie, "The Giver," really struck a nerve. These subtle and not-so-subtle messages tell us to move out to pasture and let those who are younger occupy the prime spots.

I'm not interested in providing fuel for the generational wars that are often waged in the media and in corporations. There is great value in having the creativity and energy of younger employees, or the inventiveness of the adults who grew up in the era of the internet. There is also value and worth in the experience of the older worker who can navigate the space between idealism and practicality to create influence. If you are still breathing you still have something to contribute to a life, a community, a country, or the world. The biggest obstacle to that is, ahem, us.

What can you contribute? In addition to the skills you have gained over decades of work, there are other things that make you a valuable resource today. Have you considered using the skills, knowledge and experience you have gained to pursue the direction your Internal Compass is pointing to? As we age, "The Big It" can hit differently – harder and with more force. While others may expect you to "stay down" after such a hit, you can get up. Stop for a minute and focus on what's happening in your heart: is there a strong message of "give up" there? Take a deeper breath. That heart, though wounded, is still beating. There is still life there. I invite you to consider the following stories of "getting up."

A Career Crisis

The event was my retirement from medicine after 40 years. Though the joy had gone out of patient care about fifteen years prior, I continued in practice until 2012. Then, I earned a third board certification to understand the business of medicine, so I could serve as a bridge between accountants and health professionals. Although I was no longer involved in direct patient care, I still felt like a doctor. After trying several different business positions, I realized there was nothing I could do to find joy in doctoring at any level. I also accepted that my real joy was in writing; the only reason I continued the doctor functions was to pay my editor. Even so, I hesitated until I spoke with an anesthesiologist who had retired the previous year and became a master baker. When I asked how it felt to stop doctoring after 40 years, she said, "That isn't the question. Ask yourself how you would feel if you didn't stop." A light went on in my head as I finally admitted to the damage my spirit had suffered in the years I continued in medicine past my patient care calling. The day I submitted my resignation, my spirit flew. Now when people ask me what I do, I say, "I'm a writer!"

Initially, I was elated and relieved. Though as time went on, I became stressed about the finances. Except for five years, I have worked and earned income since I was 14 years old. Not bringing home a paycheck made me feel like a squirrel pulling nuts out of my tree. It causes stress, overeating, and sometimes, paralysis. I have started to forgive myself for this and accept that one day of down time won't ruin everything.

My income dropped drastically despite the fact that I had made plans to maintain most of my lifestyle. I got more sleep and had more time to write, make contacts to improve my client base, seek professional counsel, and plan next steps. There are so many opportunities that it is sometimes overwhelming. Sometimes, I struggle to focus. I segmented my activities, so I exercise, do devotions, and write on weekday mornings. I take no meetings and read no email before noon and on weekends. This is the goal. I am still working to keep this commitment 100%. I've got about 80% now. I also simplified my closets and donated clothing, shoes, and household items I don't really need. Though I bought new jeans, otherwise, I have not replaced the items. I have gotten back to my exercise schedule and am working to manage my stress better, so I don't overeat.

If I could go back to just after the big event, I would hope to trust in my planning process more and have less stress, but the event happened only a year ago. I feel great. Though I am still nervous about finances, I realize that what I am doing will not last long enough to destabilize my long-term plan. I am confident that income will swell in the next two to five years. **– C.W.**

A Health Crisis

My event was being diagnosed with breast cancer in September 2005, at the age of 44. My life was forever changed as I mentally, physically, and spiritually prepared for the journey that was ahead of me. I experienced so many different emotions: the fear of not knowing whether I would live or die; anger and doubt; asking God why this was h happening to me while trying to keep faith and believe His words. . I was frustrated with all the doctor visits and waiting for test results and surgeries to be scheduled. My husband had to get the children to school and keep them in their normal daily routine. He cooked, cleaned, and got them off to school each day, as well as getting to the hospital daily and going to work. My sisters cooked and cleaned for me. My friends were there for my family and made sure I had everything that I needed. I couldn't work as a teacher, so my students had a substitute for almost the entire school year.

Having breast cancer made me realize that you cannot take opportunities for granted and that I must take advantage of each one that comes to me; I understand more clearly that tomorrow is not promised. I am physically and emotionally well, but I do have battle scars. They are reminders of what God brought me through and how it can be used to help others. Many women make it through but find it hard to talk about their experience. I take telling my story as part of my assignment. I AM Great, I AM HUMAN and I will remember and move forward.

Today I am part of a national sorority that I joined three years ago. As a member of that organization, I get to live out my principles of mentoring and helping young women personally and professionally. I also get to actively participate and develop sisterhood with like-minded, professional women. We help develop each other, our communities, and the next generation of women. The open book that is my life is here for others to learn from, and I continue to learn from others. — **M.E.**

A Life Crisis

Near my office desk, I had the image of a hamster…running endlessly on a glistening hamster wheel, mindlessly pursuing the helium balloon of human approval and merited favor. It was the true picture of my life irrespective of my "public face." According to the public face I stood, arms extended at the absolute zenith of my personal aspirations and professional career. But in a moment, too brief to note, God removed his hedge of protection and the beast of "Clinical Depression" roared into my life. I was surprised by the ferocity of the attack, and shocked that at age 60, after years of unrelenting battle, I had no reserve. I was spent.

I fell and did not get up. In dazed wonder, I discovered that I could not, get back up. It was not until the writing of this piece that I realized this was a seven-year journey; a journey so sudden and unplanned as to mock all future planning.

Outwardly, all was well. Daily, I exited my manicured community and took a fifteen-minute, S550 carpet ride to my custom designed office. I arrived each day, promptly at five-past, "just when I wanted to." The business had acquired a core clientele that supported both needs and extravagances.

Soon after, my untreated depression and the arrogance that a black man "don't have time to be depressed!"—began to attach to me like dust and then like quicksand. Daily, the weight of it increased imperceptibly until my moment of drowning occurred during a luncheon, later that year involving my largest strategic partner. An unplanned moment of insanity led to the loss of the relationship with my partner; the terrifying potential of imprisonment; resignation from every board or position of public leadership and contacting each key client indicating that they should find a replacement.

The unplanned moment of insanity led to the hamster exiting the wheel. Seven years later I have run the emotional gamut from mind numbing fear to reflective peace and resurrected joy. Life for me has changed my point of view: losing everything gives you a life level reset. I stopped doing what I was good at and started seeking what I was purposed to do.

Recently, I received, literally the largest "opportunity of my career" personally and professionally. I am looking at a ten-year horizon of blessing. Now when I ask myself what is most important to me, it is that I don't have to, but choose to, based on the Audience of One. – **C.H.**

In each of these stories there was a crisis that required a response. We can respond by staying down or getting up. Have you considered there is another chapter for your life that is waiting to be written? Finish the book. Don't quit before the end.

Identify the title of your next chapter. When you get up, what will you do?

_____

_____

_____

Chapter 7

The Power of the Right Question

In Chapter 2, we talked about the "Big It"; the event that knocked you down and changed your life. In my story about how the couch would have described me the two years after I lost my job as a magazine publisher, I said I would tell you what changed for me.

The day my perspective shifted was the day a former student called to ask a question that you would not ask a 'failed magazine publisher'. He asked, "Mrs. Aikens, how do you start a magazine?" What surprised me back then is that I had the answer and almost an hour's worth of surface advice. That one, rightly timed question jumpstarted the part of me that was created to help leaders and business owners, but that had gone undetected while I published magazines. I instantly saw the solution to a problem- not a magazine problem- but a 'lost people' problem.

The question identified where the needle on the compass was pointing, so I got up and followed it.

Since that day, back in 2011, there have been other twists and turns, but nothing that shook my faith – the confidence that I was able to accomplish any goal I set my heart towards. What changed? How I perceived myself changed. I had viewed myself as a failure because I didn't find a job after two years of looking. When my perception of me changed, I started the business I wanted to work for: a consulting firm that helped women over 50 to redefine themselves as owners or consultants. I put the organizational leadership master's degree to work for myself. I did the research and found out there were thousands of women – people – just like me who had been affected by the recession in 2009.

As my confidence returned, I even attempted to start another magazine. After all, it is what I knew how to do. As your confidence builds and you see new possibilities for your own life, you may be tempted to return to what is familiar – those places where you have already established competence. Follow the lessons but hold the desire to return to what was very loosely in your hands and heart. At the time I was working with a coach and realized I never wanted to start another magazine again. Why was I doing it? It was familiar, and because I was afraid to risk failure by trying something new.

Serving women like me was a cozy little niche and consulting came naturally to me. When your internal compass leads you to the right place, there is grace to accomplish what others might struggle with. The items in my toolbox took on new significance as I was able to quickly identify where an organization was weak structurally, and intuitively knew when an individual was in the wrong position. Because my targeted audience was around the same age as me, I understood the challenges of knowing there was more to do even though corporately, you were expected to "coast." I knew what it felt like to experience the heartbreak of failure and loss while knowing that your contributions were nowhere near finished. It's a beautiful contradiction and one that I could talk about and address with my eyes closed.

"Are you sure you aren't supposed to be coaching?" my own coach asked. I won't tell you how I answered, but the gist was "no." This was another important question because it addressed my comfort zone. I had become comfortable with the mechanics of consulting, i.e., "do this," or "eliminate that." However, as I sat across from accomplished leaders, I saw a recurring disconnect between the work of their hands and the compass in their hearts. I realize that sentence may be too gooey for some of you and I'm sorry, well not really.

Part of what has shut our Inner Compass down is that we don't expect to enjoy our work, and on some levels, our lives, particularly those of us from the "get the corner office generation." We were encouraged to go to school, college, if possible, find a good stable job and work hard enough to be noticed and promoted. If you had to change companies for that upwardly mobile mindset, then do so; just make sure the new situation was better or at least had the potential for better. In the background, we raised children, giving them "all the stuff we didn't get." We Boomers also divorced at higher rates than previous generations. With all of that happening, who has time to follow the "whims" of some stupid inner dream?

Yet as we age, those dreams become more insistent. We can forcibly put them away once and for all by pretending they don't exist, or we can stop and consider the rumblings of our discontented hearts. What is the problem that you are drawn to fix? When you consider that problem, what happens inside of you? Do you sense curiosity coupled with a desire to run the other way? Remember that growth doesn't happen in easy, happy places. Examine your toolbox: do you see how those tools might be tailor-made to fit that very problem? Do you see a possibility that you were made for the problem that keeps you awake at night? What are you going to do about it?

Chapter 8

Re-writing the Script

This word, script, has been buzzing around in my head for a couple of weeks. As a writer, I see scripts all around, both within myself and in the world around me. We see the results or effects of them, but the script behind is harder to discern.

A script is essentially a story, a narrative. There are four types of narrative writing according to Masterclass.com, but the one I would like to focus on is the "viewpoint narrative." In the viewpoint narrative, the story is told from different points of view. Look at this interesting note about the viewpoint script:

"This type of script allows for the possibility of an unreliable narrator, in which the person telling the story presents information subjectively and in an untrustworthy manner. The unreliable narrator is either deliberately deceptive (e.g., a noted liar or trickster) or unintentionally misguided (e.g., a middle schooler who may not fully understand the events taking place), forcing the reader to question their credibility as a storyteller. "

Coaches, ministers, friends, and loved one's bump into stories told by unreliable narrators all the time; these stories attempt to convince us of the unlikelihood of our success, the futility of our hope or the impossibility of our pursuit. Whether you are exploring a script from the natural or spiritual perspective, you must determine the origin of the script you are living, and if the narrator is unreliable or misguided.

To evaluate the script you are living, you must trace the "storyline" back to the beginning. For example, are you plagued with doubts about your ability to accomplish what you have set out to do? When did you first notice those doubts? Can you remember a time when you didn't feel doubtful? What changed? What voices, either inside or outside of you, are narrating the story you are living?

Is that narrator reliable? In the description above, the unreliable narrator can be deliberately deceptive(think about how stereotypes and discriminatory practices create a script about why certain people cannot do certain things in certain places) or unintentionally misguided (think, "How I vote makes me more righteous than you because someone I admire said so," creates a script of righteous versus unrighteous). In every story, there may be an unreliable narrator, and a biased point of view.

If you think you have been influenced by an unreliable narration of your life's story, I strongly suggest you find an unbiased source to help you uncover the truth. Those unbiased sources could be people, those who want nothing from you. Professionals who are trained to help you look at your story from a different point of view. My personal favorite is the Bible, which does not take sides and will help you identify the false scripts you have been told about yourself.

Once you have found an unbiased source, you must do the work of re-writing the script you have been living. Re-writing your life script means looking at some aspects of your life as you would a story.

For example:

- Make sure you are the leading character in your story. In every good story there is a leading character or protagonist, and the antagonist —the enemy to that character. Your story is about you, your process and your purpose as indicated by your Inner Compass. The steps to your destination will be difficult at times, but if you shrink back in fear, you could become the antagonist in your own story.

- Who are your supporting characters? Identify those people who can be trusted with your most intimate goals and hold you accountable for sticking to them. You don't need a large crowd, but three to five trusted accountability partners can help you as you re-write the script you are living.

- Don't give up because of plot twists. In every good story something unexpected happens that seems tragic and unsurmountable. However, if we continue in the story we learn that the unexpected event brings out new strength or resolve in the character. That strength and resolve actually move the story to its intended end.

- Be aware of who is "directing a scene." When you come to a conflict or a crossroad, stop and examine what is happening inside of you. Are you being directed by the voice of someone who said, "Who do you think you are to try that?" Might the director of the scene be an adult afraid to fail or look like a failure? Are your fears directing the scene, or is your sense of adventure and purpose? It's your story and you can, at any time, fire the director that doesn't suit your re-written story.

None of the other chapters matter if you don't Re-Write the Script that you are living. The possibilities for you are only limited by your ability to make the changes necessary for a new story. Get up! Let's go find what you have been missing.

Epilogue: Scavenger Hunt

I'm looking for something. I can't remember the last time I saw it, but I know it's important. Where did I put it? I scoured the files, pulling out certificates, degrees, diplomas, commendations; it wasn't there. Surely, I thought, something so important would be among my achievement documents. I'll keep looking. I walk over to the shelves where my awards are kept. Perhaps it is there. I look behind each plaque, trophy, clock, and gold-plated thingamajig. Exasperated now, I wonder where I would have put something so valuable. It feels like I have been looking for whatever this is for years. "Perhaps it is in the safe?" I reason. I check the safe at home, the safe at the bank and the safe deposit box that no one knows about. This is getting crazy. Finally, in my frustration, I sit and think, "What have I lost? What is the thing that I know is important, but that I cannot find?" I hear, in a childlike voice, "Did you look inside?"

"Inside what?!," I respond to the voice only I can hear.

"Inside here."

I pause as I catch a glimpse of childhood me, arms folded and head leaning to one side in a challenging stance.

I haven't looked there in a very long time. I understand now that the childlike enthusiasm for learning and growing is still there. Yours is still there too. It might be buried underneath years of disappointment, discouragement, and perhaps even abuse. There is a wonder and enthusiasm that you were born with, and that will direct you towards the most meaningful and purposeful experiences of your life no matter your age. You must find it though.

Here's an experiment. Find a childhood picture of yourself and try to observe what's behind the expression. I'm going to share a picture of me as a child that I have grown to love because I see me today in her posture.

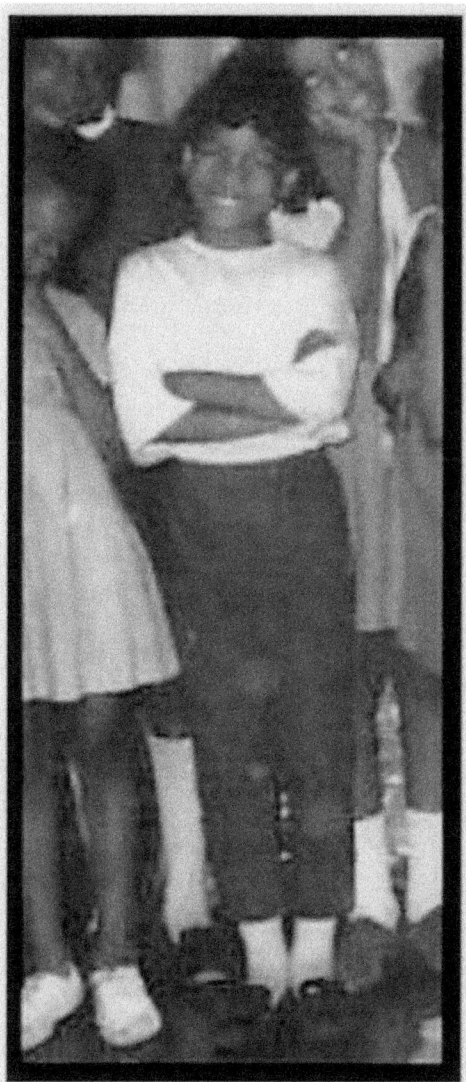

Afterword: Here for This Time

As I was reviewing the draft for this book, the George Floyd murder trial verdict was announced. I didn't realize it, but the reactions I felt upon hearing the guilty verdicts were those of someone who had been holding her emotional breath, waiting for the inevitable, in my mind, not guilty verdict. I sat there feeling blank emotionally, but aware of the havoc the adrenaline and stress hormones were wreaking on my insides. The pent-up tears stayed pent up. Needing to do something physical, I took the dog for a mile-long walk. As I considered my state, a not-so-optimistic thought invaded my consciousness, "Perhaps I am not for this time. The stress of a world at war with itself seems to assault my determined home for the best. Is this what happens when someone's time has passed?"

When we look at the events happening in our world, it may seem that your way of thinking is so vastly different, that you must be out of your time. Here's my challenge to you: As you consider the different ways you have of seeing, could you be here, in this time, to affect a new way of thinking?

Could you be the change the world is waiting for? Yes, it takes courage to face skepticism and violence with optimism and faith. Would you consider one last possibility? *Consider the possibility* that every heartbreak and battle you experienced has provided the mettle you need to live purposefully and influence real change.

Believe in the best possible outcome. Follow your internal compass. Be courageous. If you are here, this is your time.

Other Books by Michele Aikens

Not Just Any Kind of Woman

Not Just Any Kind of Woman: The Middle Years

The Homecoming:
A Story for Anyone Who Has Ever Lost His Way

Last Night I Dreamed My Purpose
(Children's Book)

Re-Writing the Script (Workbook)

www.ingramcontent.com/pod-product-compliance
Lightning Source LLC
LaVergne TN
LVHW051704080426
835511LV00017B/2730